Waiting on Rain

Jeremy Garnett

JG Poetica
2017

Copyright © Jeremy Garnett 2017

All rights reserved.

This book or any portion thereof may not be reproduced or used in any manner whatsoever without the express written permission of the publisher except for the use of brief quotations in a book review or scholarly journal.

First Printing: 25 March 2017
Edition: 1

ISBN: 978-0-9943643-2-6

Published by:
Jeremy Garnett
JG Poetica
Parcel Collect 10045 44953
44 Progress Drive
Nightcliff, NT, 0810

www.jeremygarnett.com

Dedication

To Sarah, who first awakened my realisation that my inner storm had broken its borders, and to Kelly Leviker for both the introduction and for support in those early days.

I swore, during the turmoil that followed, that my first book would be dedicated to you two.

Thank you.

Most sincerely,
and with the hope that you may one day read this, though our paths have strayed far.
Jeremy Garnett
December, 2016

To Paul Crowley, for talking me into taking a walk during daylight hours, and for continued support over the years, though we both have been through trials.

Love,

Jeremy

Contents

introduction	0
aftertaste inspiration	1
star light truth	3
cosmic questions	5
we would, so brightly burn	7
cloud dreaming	8
memories of rain	11
terror-bound	13
song of sorrow	15
lethargy awaits	17
river's flow	19
lost between	21
youtube rain	22
caught in thesaurus	23
the hardest dance of all	25
gaze, forever	27
cry of a rhythmic soul	28
eye of the storm	31
speaking with, of, god	33
ready to fall	35

0

introduction

I've lived the majority of my life in northern Australia, in the tropics, where the seasons are limited to The Wet and The Dry (both words should always be capitalised).

During The Dry, on-shore breezes wisp away the humidity until the dirt cracks, alternately baked and sodden until even the smallest hint of moisture is sucked hungrily in by any beast or bush that wanders near. In The Wet, the humidity rises, scraping like a troubled carpet across a peeling landscape until electrical friction turns the air pink, and thunderheads roll in to release their captured breath.

It is The Wet season now, and though yesterday was comparatively chilly, this early morning the is epitome of a dumpling steamer, and I, the broiling mushroom. It rained last night, pattering on the tarp above my hammock, yet not even 12 hours later, I hunger for the cooling drops as if the downpour had never been. I am addicted, and the storm is the only drug that sates the thirst. Rain to quench the hunger, and lightning to enliven the senses; a reminder from the favoured deity that the soul is indeed alive, so don't waste a single moment, or else...

This collection is a tribute to my drug of choice — my writing has been the result of many storms; physical, emotional, and spiritual. I can only hope that you realise some of the passion I taste when a wistful whim achieves an instance of phonetic perfection from thought to fact.

With much delight,
Jeremy

- - -

aftertaste inspiration

Two days rain.
Wet rotting washing hanging on the line.
On the borderline,
where tall grass meets burred grass,
pink skirted gold mushrooms
sprout from sodden ground.

A bridged creek lies empty,
rapid riches stolen by the tide.
Mud puddles crest the ridge,
an ambush.
Catching, spilling, splashing
an unaware rider;
destined to dry in the slipstream wind —
a mosquito's meal on wheels —
broiled, boiled in the sweltering sun.

Midday harks.
No shadows linger beneath high sun.
The dry dirt of a desert drought
is withered and cracking in the glare.

It rained last night?
Anyone could, would, challenge the claim,
but this is the tropics
and this day's a scorcher.

A hasty retreat from the searing air,
to sidle weary, wary, into a cavern of shadow-less floors,
sparkling in the fluro.
Breeze brushed as the air-con
strains,
growling in mechanical exasperation
as outside the trees sweat.

Shards of a broken muffin
fall,
tumbling from silvered tongs
clasped in the ring-bound fingers
of a red and black clad beauty.

Crumbling muffin and jasmine tea
unknowingly and unexpectedly
concealing the subtle taste of inspiration —
revealed within
a louvered uni cafe.

With an aftertaste of apple.

- - -

star light truth

Lying awake, staring at Scorpio,
time is as true as the stars.
We count it in breaths until we are dead
or in the turn of the seasons, and joy.

Somewhere, somehow, time began turning.
Splicing reality, spirals of clarity.
We perceive it, and this, *this* is the miracle;
that consciousness gives context to change.

Ponderous thoughts, proceed in the cold.
The winds speak of sand sucking heat.
Stars light over desert brings home perspective —
harsh is the ratio of size.

Deep the embrace that reality is,
a galaxy a sight to perceive.
We may be small in this context of all,
but joy is boundless in the wonder of life.

The night may seem dark, so deep the darkness,
when bright light catches sight in the fore,
but lying in solitude, deep in the wilderness;
darkness never could mean *alone*.

Space can be lonely, this shield from sun-fire —
the bosom of a star being scalding.
In this body of meat I like the distance
protecting from viscous plasma pools.

Distance is perspective, staring at starlight,
in the grip of a universe so harsh;
As blankets provide comfort against shiver wind,
so the universe provides solace by its nature.

- - -

cosmic questions

The Cosmos:
Spiralling outwards.
Venturing endlessly into darkness.
Spreading the realisation of time.
A child seeking knowledge of others, beyond the bounds of self-existence.

Who comprehends the one, the all?
Who is aware of the fragments, the cells?
Who has seen the planets as atoms incarnate;
wondered at the bounds of this place?

Is self-awareness a human perception?
Does the galaxy think?
Do quarks have gods they deride, incessantly cursing for cause?
Does the universe laugh?

Can you comprehend the breadth of reality?
Can reality comprehend the minuteness of you?
Does the planet itch?
Do ticks deny the eventual destruction of prey?

Do ideas choose *the person?*
Do nightmares punish the weak?
Does the knife choose the victim?
The flowers the bride?

What governs definitions?
Do neutrons see electrons as beasts?
Can you separate the dream from the dreamer?
Have you given thought to your cosmos?
Did it accept?

Thoughts break the bounds of a spiral,
caressing the heart of a stranger.
A awareness of others stills indecision,
lighting the darkness, sublime.

Self-awareness knows no distraction.
For the distracted are not self-aware.
The cosmos, itself, may have questions.
Answer truthfully, if you dare.

- - -

we would, so brightly burn

Fire fountains bloom,
beyond the icy limits of the sun.

Possibilities for expansion
are limited, by the vastness;
for heathen heat surrenders
in the embrace of solution,
and silence sunders evolution
in the constricted existence
of the void.

Where emptiness defies the mind,
in painful cries of exposition;
definition calls space empty,
and empty must be filled.

Yet destination denying properties,
as derided by religion,
call to the hearts of bold adventurers
who would journey far beyond the sun.

- - -

cloud dreaming

Shore-side —
rocks below, soon to be swept by the tide.
On the horizon the sun sets,
fading, flashing from behind the clouds.
Around me the land glimmers,
with evening dew from the retreating rain.

A lone swallow flits overhead
following the flight path of a seaplane.
Each have emerged from the storm,
flying from parts unknown.

Changing wind herds sky sheep.
Shadows and light;
sunspots in my vision create.
A blue Buddha sits in lotus
arms folded in disapproval.
His shaven head bows as I watch.

Gaze wanders and wings appear.
Larger than any creature living;
cousin to the foreseen bird —
grey feathers with bare skull of white.
An eye shifts with the breezes.
We blink together and it's gone.

Introverted mind
quickly distracted.

Cry of an unseen seagull,
halting suddenly in air mid-glide,
it sprouts leaves and drops down.
Changing, flowering, soon a tropical daffodil.
Sunflower.
Dandelion.

Remembrance of impossible birds;
Sun fire streaming over bronzed feathers,
outstretched wings,
fierce hooked beak and blazing eye.
The Phoenix soars on high,
above an abandoned supermarket.

Gripped within blackened claws,
the skeletal remains,
the rigid outstretched neck,
of a life-severed plesiosaur.
Even the sun avoids this one.

Each day a new adventure,
take a moment in between nothing.
See.

Everything exists.
Within. Without.
Imagination returned.
It was on holiday,
awaiting opportunity,
it snuck in an underground window,
and threw open old and undiscovered cupboards.

Mess. Chaos.

Fun.

- - -

memories of rain

These, the sodden days.
The windswept dripping days.

On unseen rooftops beyond the palms,
raindrops dance and slide down rusty, corrugated iron
to scatter inwards
on the veranda, and beneath,
kicking up spatters of dust,
untouched since the cyclone swept through; flooding all.

A different house; a different year, but the memories linger
called by that instant meeting of all that was and all that is.
We made boats then, from plywood, twine and corks.
Racing down the gutters,
to surf up, across the curb and get stuck in the wait-a-while

Remember
the faint sweet scent of sun-bleached earth
where orchids appear overnight, bowing homage beneath the rain.
Remember
the bitter stink of rotting palms and the mould that sprouts,
on newly painted indoor walls, fleeing from vinegar sprays.

Remember and rejoice.

Listen,
to the endless murmur of falling rain
that haunts every dream.
Listen,
as it echoes
through the wooden halls of the Queenslander,
the home of the soul

These the croaking chorus days.
The endless intermittent rainfall days.
These the nights of the flash and boom
and the dance to the *throb* of the thunder tune.

- - -

terror-bound

Curled on the couch in the heat of the day.
Its warmth a sweaty comfort,
whilst the breath of air which swirls,
unhinged by the overhead fan,
tingles, creating goosebumps.

In shadowed rooms, walls sweat
and water, born of air, remains on every breath.
Yet, for all the humid heat,
a cold sweat lingers on the brow.
Brain freeze condensation.

In the stillness,
shivering, shaking in endless loss,
despair, and swirling thoughts.
A soft harsh cry on every breath reveals
soul-bound pain, wrought by confusion.
Huddled on the couch,
seeking foetal comfort,
each struggle burrows deeper,
but the body moves only in shiver, shake.

This the storm that was never calm.
The dark shadow beneath the waves.
A cyclone amidst a camp of fragile construction,
shattering against the sandbags of artificial sanity,
until retreating, it strengthens, grows, returns.

The body, tense with half seen dreams,
keeps strangle hold on the shattered soul,
till time, breaking free of eternity,
reveals the dying sundown light.

When shivers still, the breaths grow silent
and the shaking retreats within;
till future worries reign again, or terror blows the dam.

The weight of panic rides the soul bareback,
breaking in with reality unimagined.
Until sleep consumes completely.

Too tired to dream.
Too worn to move.
Too secure in the couch.

When Morpheus beckons.
Peaceful is the sleep of the damned.

- - -

song of sorrow

Hearken, to the breeze which blows, and the words which flow, like a curlew's cry on the evening wind.
Haunting, ever haunting,
till in the fading light, gone to memory.

Listen, beneath the moon-time glow, for the dance of silent wanderers, beyond the edge of hearing,
haunting, ever haunting.
Crying out in absent loss, gone to memory.

Glance, from below shuttered eyes, as wisps of sorrow vanish between decaying buildings, forgotten trees.
Haunting, ever haunting.
A remembrance of reality, gone to memory.

Sidle out of space or time, step from reality's dream to the edge of darkness, balance on the edge that is
haunting, ever haunting
the stream of life that never was, gone to memory

Hear the curlew's cry and pirouette on the edge of silence, till truth's song cascades across the frontier,
to haunt, forever haunt,
on the periphery of existence, atop the wall of sanity, in memory's future and history's impending past.

Wait,
For the curlew's haunting cry
and weep, for all that wasn't and all that will never be,
gone to memory.

- - -

lethargy awaits

Staring beyond the hallow,
awake, lying and listening;
the vacant sounds of a city asleep
envelop, surround and bring despair.

Shadows creep across the sky.
Alone, walking the empty streets,
companionship is a lingering dream;
memory, fantasy, and soon dispersed.

Clarity floods with the dawn.
Light, pain to eyes and soul,
— curtain closes and I cry —
release, shadow-life follows fleeting.

Beauty of a friend remembered.
hope, constrained by reality.
A saxophone wails into the grey.
Unmasked, pieces of soul fly free.

Sunlight fails to awake the bleak.
Hurt, tired beyond tears,
my life continues for the simplest reason;
sanity. Thoughts cast to doubt.

Sleeping dreams provide relief;
happiness, alive between the hours.
The passing joy of full lives lived.
Woken, despair with sorrow returns.

Another sleepless night awaits.
Stories, romance read by lamplight,
are sustenance for a lonely soul.
Fictional life relieves the pain.

Night beckons beyond the glass.
Blank thoughts vanish with each step.
Lethargic cycles reign again;
Help: asked, in written confusion.

- - -

river's flow

Tears wet my eyes at the passing of time,
for time, in its passage
disturbs the motes of change
and let's loose upon the world.
History's written word.

Once, a broken soul
lay shattered,
blown asunder on storm-cycle winds
till, caught in a Savannah's raindrops
It fell. Illuminated
within the golden glow of first rains,
where tears break
across the landscape;
bringing life,
feeding hope.

Tears wet my eyes at the memory of time,
for raindrops
flow forever outwards,
gathered where the river meets the sea,
in companionship.
In joy.

While the wind is cold and sets a shiver to the skin,
our hearts, so warm,
forever
find joy within the land;
where land meets sea in celebration
and time is passing, near.

Breathe.
For every moment
deserves the breath that rises
as we watch the river flow.

Whole in heart.
Whole in mind.

We celebrate the river's flow.

- - -

lost between

Staring out the window holding my head in my hands;
the remnants of past glories hover on the edge of thoughts.
A side step, a murmur will bring history to the fore,
but pain is the icing and despair the barrier between.

Within mirrored eyes, behind unshed tears,
I remember remembering and the underlying rage.
I see a soul torn by deep regret and recognise its scars as mine.
There are no bandages that can fix a heart, its pieces scattered far between.

I look at the world and the reflection needs no glass.
Madness tears at hope's last walls, chaos dances in the veins.
Sanity is the abode of last resort, an intellectual delusion of what's right.
The sacred belief in the value of life has been corrupted,
passed-over, leaving science captured between.

Hope is an illusion, as is my reflection; each will fade when darkness takes light.
As sure as an hourglass, the future will turn, again and again, beneath skeleton hands, waiting for the silence of last.
Last breath, last existence, snuffed by bony fingers, between.

I see possibility when I look to society, to science, to the world.
Yet full with knowledge of the faults within this self,
my predictions for the future, though they flow with all fury
are best abandoned, unspoken between.

- - -

youtube rain

cold night
dry, and the fan ticks at twice speed
each blink a tick against an orb
tears pool, sting,
and the singlet I fell asleep in twists,
pulls and chokes
too cosy to strip
too lethargic to bare flesh to the fan
lying, lying, have half stripped
lying, listening to the night birds
listening for the cry of the curlew
the cry of the 'second bell, and all is well' that fails to split the tick
but gut grumbles in reply
the ache of loose screws press
built my own bed, but I ain't no Bob
no, no, no stuck in head tune,
tuning the late night radio
opening the mind
to Let Loose the internal playlist
to sink into Tunisian rock and rebellion
sweltering in DIY humidity
call me crazy, but I long for the wet
but Not Yet for the YouTube rain
tracking contortions in the writhe of the night
eyes fail to click and sleep subsumes

- - -

caught in thesaurus

I would describe her, but I have not the speech.
Beauty cannot begin, for in her eyes I see soul;
and words are but essence, in the face of the whole.
So I'm caught in thesaurus and would make a stand,
but between angelic and gracile there exists too much crude.

Thus, I've stopped short at bonny,
distracted by brilliance
and within I see brilliant;
sidestep to intelligent
and arrived hence at Truth.
Truth isn't lacking, even in essence;
yet takes breath when in presence,
and would grip my heart tight,
This in turn grasps at speech
and so in her presence,
I could sit silent all night.

Silence is a given,
though I would speak my own truth
since I've so far been incapable

For, promptly my tongue flees,
ransoms speech and emotion.
I'm left alone with devotion;
wishing only attention and a smile on her face.

Were I a worshipper of royalty,
I'd sink low to her grace.

These words yet so feeble, their stuttering hidden.
Thank goddess for drafts and scribbled, scrunched-up, revision.
Perfect testimony to the fearful state that I'm in.

All future, all possibilities, laid out before;
this enamour sparks torment, breathless and blinding.
Yet there's merit to terror,
for friendship is worth more:
so rife with discussion over ideas and delight
at life or in strife.
So,
in this life that I live, friends are unto all.
I would sooner be a friend than not know her at all.

- - -

the hardest dance of all

Hunting for the esoteric chorus.
For the rise and fall of the cymbal hum.
While the ears breathe, eyelids flutter
and the mind writhes in mental orgasm.
A shiver on the skin,
neck muscles quivering as sweat runs free from the brow.

Innocence lies in the heart of the chord,
peace on the breath,
Thoughts in flight, waiting for the crash of waves.
Till, in the turmoil of joyful emptiness,
silence is plundered by time;
whilst motion seeks existence and melody harmonises with blood.

Cold is the touch of wind on teeth bared to the moon in blunt
omnivorous pleasure.
Cast free to ride the storm that is sound.
Let Go!

The body spasms on the event horizon.
There are no limits.
There are no limitations to muscular absence.
There is only gravity.
There is only the ground.
There is only the absence of distance between the instrument and the
ear.

When the world is still, only beauty sings.

In silence, nothing is empty.
All consciousness is sound.
All sound is beauty.

Beauty is all.

Beauty is its own esoteric chorus that harmonises with existence.

With *Time*.

- - -

gaze, forever

The smiles on our faces are haunted
and though I could meet your gaze for all eternity,
you leave tomorrow
and I'm glad.

For months now, I could see the vibrations in your manner;
heart and mind throbbing in their own tune.
Out of tune; out of the local rhythm that constrains.
You were fighting that constraint, and it hurt.
So you fly away.
Body and mind, free.
Free to fly. Explore. Experience. Be!

Breathe the wind that cools the air.
Bask in the light of the moon that brightens the night.
Listen to the joy of the curlews heartbreak song,
as the sea gives life to silence.

To defy the distance, these remain.
Wherever you go, memories remain.
Wherever we are, memories clasp,
and your gaze will be with me forever.

- - -

cry of a rhythmic soul

Each word I pen,
a part of me.

Spilling, from my *Soul*.

Frothing in my unconscious being,
if bursts the bounds of mind,
crashing past the dam of *consciousness*,
flowing past fingers and into the ink of the pen.
It hits the paper;
twisting in a medley
of mutating growth.
Pulling moisture from my lips;
flourishing in the ears of strangers.

Exhibitionist;
I am
a *Performer*.

Brazen,
Stock steady in the eyes of attention.
stuttering,
shuddering,
fighting back the moths that flutter inside;
that rise, in harried flight,
in the spotlight of the stage.

As the mind huddles,
the body *speaks* —

In a cadence,
that dances to the written rhythm of the words;
to the rhythm of the soul,
the rhythm of the world.

As a moth to a flame,
or bare dirt under *rain;*
there's a *need*
and a *calling*
and a *summons*
in the words,
that creeps through the cracks
in the shell around the soul.

A thrumming in the rhythm,
and a shiver in the call,
that sets the head to nodding,
and the boot to tapping of the floor.

There's a hunger for connection,
crying out from under all;
waiting for emotion,
in the faces of the crowd.

Till reflection in their eyes,
resounding out of darkness,
sets the heart to dancing;
waking up the consciousness,
and setting it to stand.

Fast and *Proud* and *Glorious!*

In this forest of companionship,
On the stage that is the world.

- - -

eye of the storm

Cyclonic dreams,
held firm between anticipation
and the spiral of creation;
summoned by constant
longing in the beat of the heart.

Harmonious,
lyrical discord
shatters the perception of a caged existence
till the twisting movements
of musical freedom
wrest control of the dance.

The instantaneous flicker of
soundwaves
cascading off the eardrums of air-con vents
spark muscular chaos
beneath the thrumming
thoughts of the band.

Shuttered eyes face inwards
whilst the murmur of humanity —
The swirling breath of life entwined —
brings peace
through silence.

Adrenaline sings
as the dance in the eye of the music continues;
whilst outside, windblown leaves
celebrate their own twisted freedom.
As the storm beckons.

- - -

speaking with, of, god

Speaking with, of, God
I saw the *rise*, the *downfall* of the race
That *we*, who became, who broke —
exist; only in the breath another does not breathe.

Unable to run, I cannot but rant
as the consistent inconsistencies:
of doubt, of faith;
of rebellion, of acceptance;
of the guilt and free will
that plague the youth and the dying,
casting them into the light.

We, the self and the mirror, haunt.
A cultural exchange of disgust.
A sharing of spirit that rends.
Till we tear each other in twain
seeking solace in the blood of the slain —
splashing pretty patterns on the walls if only to distract from the pain.
All for selfish gain.

Till the dinner bell tolls 'reminder'
and we're caught starving midst the gore
with Reason banging on our noggins saying
"Tomorrow there'll be more.
Go wash your hand before eating.
After supper we'll play Peace.
It's like Patience only more diverting,
for Delusion deals a righteous hand."

Now I'm at the sink and staring
I've met God's gaze beyond the glass.
One of us is weeping
and we speak as if for days.

Till I wash my hands in Purity;
salty tears to clean the stain.
Pull the plug and turn away,
seeking supper and the game.

- - -

ready to fall

Riding the dog into the wind.

On the horizon, blue water is cut —
Mandorah has fallen off the edge.
Spots on my face remind of missed sleep
and too much time spent in storage sheds.

Waiting not for the rain —
 It is already knocking.
But for the shower's cleanse of moving dust,
and the grime of memory.

The horizon approaches.

Done moving,
I am ready to fall.

- - -

www.ingramcontent.com/pod-product-compliance
Lightning Source LLC
Chambersburg PA
CBHW062004180426
43198CB00036B/2367